D1606778

Consent

by Jayneen Sanders

illustrated by Cherie Zamazing

Consent
Educate2Empower Publishing an imprint of
UpLoad Publishing Pty Ltd
Victoria Australia
www.upload.com.au

First published in 2021

Written by Jayneen Sanders
Illustrations by Cherie Zamazing

Designed by Stephanie Spartels, Studio Spartels

ISBN: 9781761160233 (hbk) 9781761160097 (pbk)

A catalogue record for this
book is available from the
National Library of Australia

Disclaimer: The information in this book is advice only, written by the author based on
her advocacy in this area, and her experience working with children as a classroom teacher
and mother. The information is not meant to be a substitute for professional advice. If you
are concerned about a child's behavior seek professional help.

Using Little **BIG** Chats

The *Little BIG Chats* series has been written to assist parents, caregivers and educators to have open and age-appropriate conversations with young children around crucial, and yet at times, 'tough' topics. And what better way than using children's picture books! Some pages will have questions for your child to interact with and discuss. Feel free to use these questions and the Discussion Questions provided on page 19 of this book to help you assist your child with the topic being explored. Stop at any time to unpack the text together; and try to follow your child's lead wherever that conversation may take you! So, please, get comfy and start some empowering 'chats' around some BIG topics with your child.

The Body Safety titles should ideally be read in the following order:
Consent, *My Safety Network*, *My Early Warning Signs*,
Private Parts are Private, and *Secrets and Surprises*.
The remaining titles can be read in any order.

Meet the Little **BIG** Chats KIDS

Theodore

Asha

Ardie

Tom

Jun

Jamie

Belle

Lisa

Maisy

Tilly

Maya

Ben

Hi! I'm Theodore.
Today we're learning
about consent.

This is my body.

It belongs to me!

I have a body boundary.

This is the invisible space
around my body.

And even though you can't
see my body boundary,
it's STILL there.

CAN YOU SHOW
ME YOUR BODY
BOUNDARY?

No one can come inside
my body boundary.

They have to ask me first.

I can say 'Yes'
or I can say 'No'.

Can I have a kiss?

10

No, thanks.
But I can
give you
a hi-five!

Consent is a special word.

It means I have HAPPILY said 'Yes' to someone coming inside my body boundary.

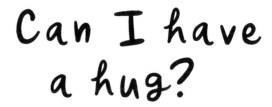

Yes,
you can.

Sometimes I feel
like a hug or a kiss
and sometimes I don't!

I can say 'No' to hugs and
kisses and that's okay.

This means I have NOT
given my consent.

I can give a hi-five or
bump elbows instead.

It's always MY choice!

This is my body.

I can say 'Yes' or I can say 'No' to someone coming inside my body boundary.

I am the boss of my body.

My body belongs to me!

WHO IS THE BOSS
OF YOUR BODY?

DISCUSSION QUESTIONS
for Parents, Caregivers and Educators

The following Discussion Questions are intended as a guide, and can be used to initiate open, age-appropriate and empowering conversations with your child.

This book is a simple introduction to consent and a child's right to their own personal space, also known as their body boundary or body bubble. Begin consent education early by asking for your child's consent and explaining to them what you are doing as you interact together, and why. For example, 'Can I hold your hand? I'm doing this so we can safely walk together across the road.' Wherever possible allow your child body autonomy.

Page 5
Introduce Theodore. Ask, 'What do you think "consent" might mean?'

Pages 6-7
After reading the text, you may like to extend the conversation to talk about what your child likes about themselves, and all the wonderful things their body helps them to do. Your child may also like to draw a picture of themselves.

Pages 8-9
Ask, 'What do you think invisible means?' Have your child stand up tall, and with their finger, draw around their body boundary. You could draw around yours, too!

Pages 10-11
Explain to your child that because their body belongs to them, they have the right to say 'Yes' or 'No' to people coming inside their body boundary. Note: this relates not only to greetings, for example, ask your child, 'Can someone come inside your body boundary and take your hand without asking? Can someone tickle you without asking?' Note: in relation to 'tickling games', if a child consents and then says 'Stop'; the 'tickler' must stop. Consent can be withdrawn at any time.

Pages 12-13
Ensure your child understands that people need to ask for hugs and kisses, holding hands, tickling games, etc. Also, ensure that friends and family know they need to ask your child for their consent whenever they come inside their body boundary. Note: medical professionals need to ask for your child's consent when examining their body; this includes a dentist looking inside your child's mouth.

Pages 14-15
Ask, 'Is it okay to say "No" to a hug or a kiss from an adult? How about a teenager or another child?'

What other ways can you greet someone?' Other ways to greet: blow a kiss, shake hands, wave, hi-five, bump elbows. You may have your own special family greetings.

Pages 16-17
Ask, 'Do you think this little girl asked Theodore for a hug? Did she ask for his consent? What do you think Theodore said? How do you know he said "Yes"? How is Theodore choosing to greet the other child?'

Page 18
Have your child stand tall and proud, just like Theodore, and say loudly, 'I am the boss of my body. It belongs to me!'

For more in-depth books on consent, see Jayneen Sanders' children's books 'Let's Talk About Body Boundaries, Consent and Respect', 'No Means No!' and 'My Body! What I Say Goes!'

Little BIG Chats

A series of 12 little books to help kids unpack BIG topics

Consent
Introducing consent and body boundaries
by Jayneen Sanders   Illustrated by Cherie Zamazing

Secrets and Surprises
Learning the difference between secrets and surprises
by Jayneen Sanders   Illustrated by Cherie Zamazing

Private Parts are Private
Learning private parts are private and what to do if touched inappropriately
by Jayneen Sanders   Illustrated by Cherie Zamazing

My Safety Network
Introducing a Safety Network (3 to 5 trusted adults a child can go to if they feel unsafe)
by Jayneen Sanders   Illustrated by Cherie Zamazing

My Early Warning Signs
Exploring Early Warning Signs and what to do if a child experiences these signs
by Jayneen Sanders   Illustrated by Cherie Zamazing

Families
Celebrating diversity in families
by Jayneen Sanders   Illustrated by Cherie Zamazing

I Always Try
Developing a growth mindset of resilience and persistence
by Jayneen Sanders   Illustrated by Cherie Zamazing

Feelings
Understanding different feelings and emotions
by Jayneen Sanders   Illustrated by Cherie Zamazing

Everyone is Equal
Introducing the importance of gender equality and diversity
by Jayneen Sanders   Illustrated by Cherie Zamazing

Empathy
Exploring the meaning of empathy and kindness
by Jayneen Sanders   Illustrated by Cherie Zamazing

Mindfulness
Exploring the importance of mindfulness and learning calming skills
by Jayneen Sanders   Illustrated by Cherie Zamazing

Around the World
Celebrating racial equality and diversity
by Jayneen Sanders   Illustrated by Cherie Zamazing

Milton Keynes UK
Ingram Content Group UK Ltd.
UKHW051857051224
3359UKWH00009B/36